FALSE SPRING

FALSE SPRING

Amie Zimmerman

New York

ISBN: 979-8-9915011-7-0
Library of Congress Control Number: 2025946526

Cover art by alya ansari
Book design by Deborah Thomas

NEW YORK STATE OF OPPORTUNITY | Council on the Arts

This book is made possible, in part, by the New York State Council on the Arts with the support of the office of the Governor and the New York State Legislature.

Roof Books are published by
Segue Foundation
300 Bowery FL 2
New York, NY 10012
seguefoundation.com

For the complete Roof catalog, go to:
Roofbooks.com
Roof Books are distributed by
Independent Publishers Group
IPGbook.com

Contents

I.

II.

III.

I.

false spring

careful
taking is a matter
of reckoning

we who know exceptions when we see them

we who have married
the enemy exactly

to watch them die young

calm down, I said

soft footed
we readied for the raids, ahead—

snitch tongues
pious

and grieving our lack
of mercy

untitled

dominion has taken me
I am Its

waiting
the nature of bondage changes

blood simple

reframing my weakening into faultlessness

to resign oneself
to who one really is

the air in that!

shave my head and leave the foot
just standing there

Walter Benjamin

A child is an ongoing cataclysm of the future self.

I'm ambivalent about the prohibition

on encountering my past self during time travel.

If I don't die, the clamoring second choice

is the most basic of nature poems. The danger affects

both the content of the tradition and its receivers.

Straight line elegance is no guarantee: clumsy work matters.

What's the correct instinctual reaction to brake lights.

God knows my beacon is loud and rumpled.

I meant what's the correct institutional animal.

Strapped to the present I find cyclically diminishing

attachment to my lover, the only thing I can't let go.

Have I in a sense *moved my fashion* forward.

Nothing is pending.

Chronology being therefore useless

we are an immaculate—beholden—historicity.

entry

there is some confusion about the use of we. how it started. damp woods are a we. calico cats are a we. driving to Las Cruces in the naugahyde backseat windows down in summer is a we. we is automatically historical, yes, and becoming the number of bosses we've had now that we're never not begging; the pivot of love from that which is seen to that which is eaten. now is as good a time as any to learn to graft. forsythia is a we. dianthus is a we. cotoneaster whose berries feed the robin is a we. viburnum drowning in aphids is a we. spiraea a we. crocosmia a we. hellebores a we. cultivate anger as a way to direct the piss away from our own feet. aging out again. again into the thickness of life beyond young hope. pull up the floorboards. naming is a function of we. we are still in love and attest to existence as all that is. we woke from the dream of our feet battered by rolling rocks in the tide, our bodies arching into the forest. ask how far how far how far back.

false spring

this war is a real war
voting can't fix

if we organize around the kindness principle
we'll get bullets in our eyes

we'll get bullets anyhow
there's a few in my hand right now

Walter Benjamin

one could say
have faith & mean
            we're dead anyway

we are a messianic creature—
            meaning eludes me too

above silence there is work
the branching word obliterated by its sentence

reform is the site of reified harm
            the horror of *this* continuing unchecked
            into acquiescence

— where is the fulfillment of the material promise
            are we still waiting for any day

untitled

to be certain I am
a petty war beast

panicked, lowing

birthing babies others rescue off the ground
before my mother hoofs can stomp them

I am sweetly drunk and dewy
to quote: I mean to be a terror to the world

we can end this now
skate through the intersection without looking

is this a goddamn revelation of self, or what

gather around me, fathers
raise me up so I can see

entry

this sense of before and after is doctrine. as if truth is formation / event / conclusion. *the lilies were lost in a freak hailstorm.* nobody wakes up streaked white from a shock; that's just not science. we are hypocrites with our diamond ring commitments. dehydrated tongues wagging, ready to lick the next vacated seat. accounting for fuzzy time, blackout fucking, grease in the bed. possess more than we need. politicization of self that expands and contracts to meet social fashion and function. *run to the end of the block and back.* light a smoke. that fifth cost seven dollars. fifth that seven-dollar cost. dollar cost that seven fifth. cost that fifth dollar seven. dollar. drowning in the greater meaning of me. now is not the time for empty threats; you better chop that head clean off.

untitled

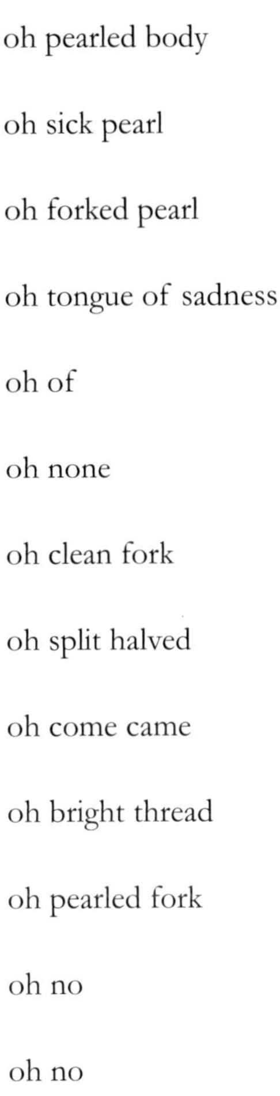

oh pearled body

oh sick pearl

oh forked pearl

oh tongue of sadness

oh of

oh none

oh clean fork

oh split halved

oh come came

oh bright thread

oh pearled fork

oh no

oh no

false spring

flank the side
as if we are losing all

and we are
gross as it is to eat our own

baby liver is adult liver
only smaller less sexy

what are clouds in a catastrophic flood

think of the deaths:
first concrete, then the mystery, the shatter,
the fire

hunger in the valley, stalking

entry

for the vow bring copper. time is recorded by what noise our ears distinguish, length of echo. if here, it means we have begun the signature. feet in mucky shore, squat for heron, for dragonfly, for sweet sturgeon. unbuckle palm and draw out pollen. reach for the rock and bash through sternum, tired of anything resistant. remember shoppers who took pictures, who could not look. remember aura of their fascination. when the bars bent, though, we stayed. waited to be gathered. mud stirs in waters at the headway, eagles watch glass folding in bonfire. break off my calf, eat first the heel. to remain to remain is joy to remain. mouth a tunnel of praise.

inside this house negotiate numerous covenants: take out the bins, buy things, exterminate vermin, feed ourselves and others, party until we cannot see, eat facing the tv. who gains the yoke of covenant now, holding out soft cups of organs? flood takes the garden, river inches closer to foundation. shuffle through the house where all covenants stand, toenails scraping floorboards, hair brushing the ceiling, so dense, use butter to squeeze between bodies. it takes an hour to get to the bathroom. extenuating life.

mouth a whetting stone, open sternum a reservoir for oil. vehicle a ladder for new fish to climb. mouth a tunnel of praise growing wider than the river, gold vein, geyser, face the peeled back lily, sound outshined in the shriek of collective loss, engulfing wartime music on speaker in wartime factory, forever boat endlessly bailed.

false spring

wherein anger is the short supply in a long puzzle, shaving of
corners leaves no way

to enact the assumption, we might want to bludgeon the works
just as well

volcanic craters, provided enough time, blossom again with
visible life suddenly what viable

risk

we gather spent ordnance stacking in secret as evidence that we
cost them something

false spring

if wages are our primed
        dead labor
        & work

is the measure of how hard
        one's dick gets

for the worst thing not
        happening, then how

ungrateful we seem
        to be physically fighting

our enemies & yet this suspended
        path contains a wideness still

hemmed in violence, where my life
        is in our hands not theirs

Surplus

When I say I hate cops I mean I hate cops.
 To mutter this means nothing.
  To write a poem or a paper changes
  little—I am not fooled.

We all have sets of choices.

I'm chopping off my hand to have something to throw.
 I need that hand to work.

I had no idea you were so flammable waving like a pinwheel
in the street.

Encountering tension only feels like thickness.
 Brutality is matchstick brittle, snapped
 elasticity—rubber with no sting; falling insides
 blunted; lack of containment.

The university president criticized me for invoking suffering
metaphorically then walked away when I told him about the
going price of plasma.

Ice in the shape of me moves like I move.
 Removes distinction except when you squint your
 eyes. I'm still there somewhere.

I reach out in love so many times.

The bank won't give me laundry quarters: coin shortage is a
weird sort of precarity.

Our grave errors are sunflowers so heavy with seed they
break their own necks.

The chief of staff asked what he could do to help so we hung
ourselves. Be here when I get back from my shift.

An hour-long conversation about the shade of yellow is
normal.
          Abnormality as a concept can go fuck itself.

Identifiers have so much slippage.
          Claiming is likewise un/important.

I could have been carrying flowers and he still would have
punched me.
          I would like to punch someone while holding flowers.
                    A colorful and sweet-smelling punch.

Neurological constructivism negates objective truth.
          Concern for how HR perceives work-life balance.
                    Where is the collaborative meaning-making
                    in payroll.

Sometimes my poems feel like a transcript—

There are limits to negotiated disgust.

Whale calls nestled inside my radiator's ribs.
          When have I become an urbanity.

I imagine waste lingering inside my body.
          Frottage between the mileage of my intestines the site
          of transference. Dead touches the dead. I grow dim
          with exposure.

Tonight I will again forget how miserable it is to wake up.

Perspicuousness.

I cried in the finance office.
She was struggling with the ethics
of acknowledgement.
My responsibility to perform a plausible
narrative. The institution demands
to be wooed.

Please look at my teeth.
No one has in so long.

I don't mind a catalog of your boring life as long as you don't try to teach me something.
The deal's off. Probably 12 years ago.
Presumably the reason I can't remember is
because it was so boring. All I ask is to remain
in undisturbed boredom.

The test is who shows up.

Discipline is frolicking on the play structure now.
New parents have the best ideas.

Flowers don't all deserve to live.
I desire to feel, but for one week.

The corroborative nature of ________ as it relates to *meaning*.

Eat a bag of dicks, thoughtfully.
Acquiesce to the debt of life.

Far away I see the wave of knowledge crawling slowly and throw up in fear.

How easily codes are violated; how easy to omit the related cause for sanctions; how now I must meet with Craig to determine my fate.
O Craig! Succor!

The finished project is ugly.
The process sublimned panic for a few hours but now
I continue increasing its size hoping to love what I
have made, adding instead to the size of my panic.

If by open you mean an amount, they have not built a structure large enough.
If by amount you mean solution, open
the bags of skin.

untitled

The circle I walk around the mountain laurel now has infinity
    of my bodies following my bodies, walking blisters

filling with water. I could drink my blister. Mountain laurel
    is fed by flies when everyone swore they were bees.

Why am I following you up these stairs again. The building of
    small bodies of combustibility, smaller rooms

so the flames can move faster each time. My heart is leaping
    out of me. I have leapt off expecting to die

instead there is only blister water, infinite bodies on infinite
    stairs, purple, flies, and thirst. How do I give up
    wanting this. I don't.

Walter Benjamin

I remember practicing for pain by holding ice cubes
our need for each other outweighs the potential, not
actual, harm; hold ground for a specific cause beyond
the minutes of my lifespan; waiting behind the wall
we crouched holding hands breathing hard; I am still
too desperate for ennui; can we rethink *desire for*
difficulty as inhabiting excellence; pursuit of self is
eased by looking up; I'm still searching; sliding into a
slump on the ground feels better than posture; the
boba tea of redemption requires a special straw;
separating holiness from religion until there is only
lightning; your version and mine are different;
compromise can be a form of domination; my
preference is to be a giant brick of love

untitled

struck, the stone
carries its mark

false spring

wind carried the soft chant

of feet today – I stood working

hundreds passed

I heard each toe land & knee crack

& flexed my ankles in solidarity

we say we see the lifting fog

rolling back over buildings or fields

oh but what we finally see is us

the street is not a metaphor

what is the measure of here
here

long tilts of sun
separated from noise by birdsong
pounding of the local piston
distraction of life from work

radiators pop
all those mice on the other side of the wall

a person can admire prettiness and at day's end
recognize a parasite

each time money
creates the unbearable
there are those who can't wait to be born

people embarrassed by the wrong things
work, its valor, pried from the worker
root, stem, and fruit
of immaculate means

cultivated grass, not worth the water

submerged by perception, my body like a body
streaming light
is fed

is feeding
wheels without grip

fear is lust
idol worship, curated, chanting from mouths full of
healthy, original teeth
not for battle but for battle hardiness in this
soft age

lawn
torches, given numbers, will light up
green twigs freshly harvested

who hungers for revolution
carries an imagined self as shield

tell me I don't recognize the polo shirt buttoned to the top
wave your flag
wave it

people embarrassed to name their relation to poverty
is to be embarrassed by—hear me out—a construct

none of us who work a shift
know the truly wealthy

exhausted by glory captured
toward shoulder

arm crook
kettled and black with
flame

the messenger is awake with opening
breath flame-blacked throat

that crook

that
was the signal

sweep away all but spirit
drown goodness
the eye seeks an embarrassment of virtue

the door hung high swings
shutter of light, bringer of lunacy
of lunar silence

not wind, not ocean, but the hundreds of wings settling, arrival
to what has been called

drunkard falling from his stopped car it is 4am, we are
witness to each other in the startled street

all day waiting for the sun
we lay in the street and drown in virtue
many in God's water what to drown

who crushes us with desire imperious
crushed where we lay

on the ground

I am overrun I have been visitation
the ground

our bodies are starling motion on the ground
street is the starling, the call is the witness,
poverty is the relation
shield is not a language object,
it is a street object

on sacred pavement

recite belief
from our memories, crooks and black throats kettled

I know what we are : : please don't make me do this
: need to move

: move or I'll

: use this if

: doing is illegal

: been declared

: illegal : use force

: declare this

: disperse, you

: must disperse : the crowd : we will : means necessary
: authorize : you : you : : :

the ground, our feet are starlings   and
gift of flame

zero
        sons of fortune   many-eyed seraph of 3rd &
                                   Madison

we know the promise is to uphold property
        in service of wealth; we cannot name our
        embarrassment
                drunk, stumbling witness in the street

the street is not a metaphor

what is the value of here
here

some people argue negligible harm resides with the individual
collective accountability therefore is truly
revolutionary

bonfire of wealth, they must at last
gaze upon each other as kindling

~~wealth is not constitutive of collective~~ wealth is
inherently solitary
enacted upon the collective

sons of embarrassed fortune, come at me
flock of starling, disperse

thump the ground raw with quaking piston
love is not a leveler
a commoner's sutra
it is recognition
is witness

sense of binding, beating crooked
emerge from earth's center not looking right or left
dead run
bring them down to the street
call them down

there is no natural order but what we establish, drowned in spirit
within the ecstasy of movement

we are not bound to enact reverse domination
do not believe false prophets

if you live I live
this is not a metastatement
it is atonement in every sense

property signals security but that can be found in many ways
hey crook hey throat hey black night
swallowing
the flock

what is the loss of place or people what is our us

false spring

hate is the stranger hunger of the two

photographs of people
are photos of the wane

it's a map, really
the luster of burnished opinion

our bloody tampons as weapons, remember?

place a piece of crash glass
in every bespoke mailbox as a warning

your space is not your own; we'll break
the necks of all our chickens to waste the life we have

what won't we do if the goal
is to pretend we can be bloodless

untitled

all trains are dead trains
    moving in the same direction.

a phalanx of stoned wind
    bored of talk
    stuffs your mouth with its hand.

there. there is the quiet of winter
    the suicide of February
    you've been trying to avoid.

the weight of people is clear glass
    shattering with every step.

the city tells us we are not natural.

we think we've stopped
    leaving babies in the forest.

drinking our own water
    dense with people weight
    sticky with people.

we will die by doing so
    and also die by not.

Filmic

With a kind of treelike virtue
I sent my soldiers to your side

Pregnant once a year
For the sake of losing what's mine

Posthole diggers dig post holes

Shimmering lights suggest the spiritual
Filmic befriending of violence

What occurs: cutaway freedom
Staged in the wolf den coup

My enemy wraps life in death cloth
I trundle behind making snips where I can

Admit it; the gore makes sense
Bleeders are the best friends

Break it like a hook

Like a waxwing in a dogwood
Sentimental and pink

Like the loss of body
Is the only real loss

untitled

The first half of any day is spent vibrating with the sound of recycling bodies.

If you don't know how to listen, whatever god says is what you must do.

Three generations became glue today. It smelled like nothing. No one noticed.

Finding out you loved someone enough to become sick for them.

Plants, inimitably, still grow as long as there is something resembling soil.

The second half is spent eating what we grow if we know how to bow down.

Choose the midpoint. Choose what hosiery can be the most tightly wound.

A number of eyeballs make broth for soup. That actually did smell good.

The whole day is spent waving goodbye to people marching in the street.

Goodbye. Goodbye. Goodbye. I love you all. Limited adhesion glue.

The last footage of me is my fingernails becoming trees. The grove exists.

Neighborhoods of a future age in which I am a soft ghost in the canopy.

entry

a while back the secret whispered itself and became flesh. how we worked became seed but the seed was dust. at night lasers shot straight into the sky while we crowded together bending our necks, the sources searing our eyes. patterns in the cloud cover resembled mandala. mothers mothered too much. we did not dance. we saw the shore receding, land moved because we moved it. what erupted from the mouth were shoes. potato vines bore buried knife spores, the trees fruited fuzzy tiny semi-automatics. we used hot glue guns to affix currency to our skin, we shone.

shallow sprinkles of water. roots grow to the surface and then —shuuuuff—blown over by the softest breath. our language is like that sometimes. the contradictory necessity, parasitic semiotics. holdover where there is a state, culture to have a face. language puts names to faces. we think we are such revolutionaries.

dowry

standing in a crowd the betrayal is the crowd   there isn't
the beginning we thought
          there was when we first began to walk.

bluegrass filters to the violet light inside   sound was
the answer before turning to light when sound became
          too violent, before violence also became equivocal.

where I am watching you & you watch   the blank wall
longing is associated with
          weakness & a willingness to sell but everyone I know
          feels it anyway.

I wanted a single warm body, mine.

closing doors, closing cabinets, turning doorknobs, the sun
found its way
          world-making depends upon our narratives.

we've hunted many things as dowry, earned, thinking of the
work   strobe as light echo as series of unique marks when
witnessed, the filter of the eye creates the watermark.

paid five then five then five more   hardening as a
metaphor
          elliptical reasoning answers or doesn't answer the
          question of what we consider soft.

tell me you love me & they will love me too, the crowd
suppression of the self   works only so long
          it will come back—emphasize—with a vengeance.

this grip is too hard a grip.

I cannot be what connects the fool to his foolishness
the goal, remember, is to pass through
which feels like the definition of suffering or why it's
said to be necessary.

the day, when it ends, chopped & rung.

II.

Author's note:
Several years ago, I began writing a series of poems in response to the work of Korean poet Kim Hyesoon, taking up themes of abjection, the absurd, the celebrity of poets, poetic ideals, and transactional social relations. Eventually I selected seventeen of the poems and used a randomizing formula to re-order the lines, narrowing by choosing numerically rotating lines. "On the Nature of Bondage" is the resulting constraint-based experiment, in which I limited the interventions to minor punctuation and white space arrangement to highlight the disjunctive qualities of disordered lines. Several of these poems appear in their original state as "untitled" in this collection, although not all the "untitled" are part of the experiment.

On the Nature of Bondage

the train that runs over a dog

if performative, objection is to the binary choice

with no pants on

I am Its

blood simple

shave my head and leave the foot

petty war beast

to quote: I mean to be a terror to the world

is this a goddamn revelation of self, or what

in all things

recognize falsehood:

I haven't bothered to crack that one yet

on the wall is hung a man

reaching over your living head

I am here, if I must, to suffer

//let me step in front of me

//let me take my bullet

//let me love unremittingly myself

//let me unlock my own potential

//let me fail myself

//let me know my true nature

//let me be there when I die

a cheater

lying on my belly in their St. Augustine

forgive me,   forgive me

for *death*   so that he knows I'm thinking of him

I'm not out here listening forlornly to birds

it's like my vagina penis can't get enough

I mean it's everywhere all the time

—the bloom of knowledge that follows—

I needed to lie and to grieve the lie as well

selfish sex can be the only contract

do I lie? or

stiff   marble

the sick source of all desire

( ) oh of

( ) oh clean fork

( ) oh no

raw possession

what a disappointment I could not

more readily

contract a way to measure myself

my harness, but publicly instead

satisfying diminishment, as I'd expect

( ) oh clean fork oh split halved oh come came oh bright
thread

( ) oh sacred thigh oh swish oh swi— oh laundry basket

( ) oh meat of sickness oh irritating bystander

my unending desire for your unending desire for me

dear satellite

divorced in the meantime absolution of the royal we

I am not who I thought I was

any other significancy

specifically the raw meat stage

like every time you orgasm, the animal is skinned

lick frosting deep in each other's eyes

the nature of bondage changes

to who one really is

birthing babies others rescue off the ground

—we can end this now—

open weeping can appear to be

a virus gone systemic

hold me under

the beetle's language is tongue and groove

the boring beyond:

//a family portrait of me

//falsely accusing myself

//in the night I will come for me

//let me give to me more than I receive

//let me donate my kidney to me

in the presence of ripened nectarine

tongue softly in the dirt

I leave trifles around the house

my own edification

of fucking someone

an embarrassment of riches

as if I could feed a waiting crowd

I wanted you to tell me what you wanted

to know the truth before it is plain

( ) oh pearled body

( ) oh none

( ) oh bright thread

I kept expecting it to get better

suck you into   me

provide you into   providing   me

fair bleaching weather exposure // pregnant but only
the early stages

( ) oh tongue of sadness oh of oh licked asshole oh none

( ) oh meat bird oh weekend traveler oh time turned

coarse whine   an elaborate

think about fucking you all day long   think about

rutting dogs on an endless loop   weapon of safety

brick upon hard noise

halfmehalvemehaveme

you   love, one you   know

I'll get what I want

reframing my weakening into faultlessness

panicked, lowing

skate through the intersection without looking

I know enough theory

love

teeth   snapping at my soft under arm

a dull degradation: the self as sole witness

//let me find the happiness I so richly deserve

//let me pay my own bills

//let me deeply grieve the absence of me

the story told for infinity

sex is not about sex

I imagine encountering one would

when I say no one is talking about the grief

the moment between the fist lands

would happen so and so

rose haze

() oh forked pearl of sickness

() oh split halved

anal is, a priori, useful

so you could feel

where the phantasy enacts

a shadow birthed and eaten

() oh boulders of empathy oh bright tongue oh stroke

—only what is in front of me is what I admire in you—

my gaping thinning

train that is the only way to orgasm, killing an animal

let's eat cupcakes at each other
the air in that!

before my mother hoofs can stomp them

all things

with a bit of leather between my teeth

against your herky bladework

//let me be the lover of my dreams

//where I am the center of my universe

//in the dark about my own motivations

it is the smell I recognize

which set in motion some complex emotions for *death*, too

the relief of uncoupling too obvious

to suckle the child—to feel my body multiply

new—reliable only in newness

( ) oh tongue of sadness

teeth in   to the gums

more resistance

small thing like the sun

( ) oh dull brightness oh bright fade oh fate oh hum hum hum

my cock all day   abandonment is the false positive

let my strength carry you

the first few days together

buy gold chains off the internet without breaking gaze

to be certain I am

raise me up so I can see

like a beetle's curl and splay

//let it be me

//let me meditate on myself

//watching me when I sleep

no one stops getting hungry

hackles become a form of welcoming

then I knew I didn't want it after all

pattern, completed replication

() oh no

the fool's construct:

() oh pearled fork oh no oh no oh turned signal oh turn

() oh laundered extinction oh halved oh sacred brine

to unsatisfactory margins

or even a stranger, killing a stranger dog

just standing there

a house, cursed, is a distraction

depinioned, what will you do now, O man?

//it wasn't mine to have

one day when I leave the house

in usefulness, use should be pronounced

you said, sculptor that you are

() oh sick pearl

I wouldn't bleed

how simple it is to wait forever

your no a secular investment in holiness

I don't believe myself I believe

to resign oneself

should be denied agency

//let it center on me

//contractually obligated to me

this murderous anonymity

do I lie?

so

() oh pearled body oh sick pearl oh forked pearl of sickness

I’ve smeared blood on Mondrian

                    dominion has taken me

                    whose arms and legs

          //let me pick me out of a lineup of me

          with a hard and slippery ‘*zz*’ sound

the accident of age

against celebrity

asking can you feel   soft reduction, the measurement of
which

                              I am sweetly drunk and dewy

                    beside—how one does with others

          struck, the stone carries its mark

( ) oh licked asshole

( ) oh clean street oh split fork oh facile ending oh slop

          we are missing the point of the dilemma

          //it all comes down to me

I wanted to grieve   the way I wanted to fuck

( ) oh straight shift oh extinct clam oh irritant oh street

          waiting

out into the neighbor's field

( ) oh pearled fork

every day the loop of isolation tightens

the truth is, the truth is too simple for what happened

—gather around me, fathers—

( ) oh come came

by this I mean how we act

is more exciting that way in your hand the real thing

//I should be ashamed of myself

site of entry to constricted certainty

let me drip the self miserly

III.

Mother

One day I had a kid

Someone said
    Now you know
    how to love something
    more than yourself

Then I walked around
and said
    You should learn
    how to love something
    more than yourself

false spring

the nights there's riot in the air
I'm finding what's possible hidden inside
an ability to go unrecognized

like when someone tells me to vote
my conscience but living where I do
I'm finding hard rhetoric an answer
that staunches the erosion of ethics

every person is someone I could kiss
full on the mouth & get away with it

we know what isn't a lie because we've loved this way

untitled

to know the truth before it is plain
stiff marble

new—reliable only in newness

rose haze
the accident of age

pattern completed, replication
the sick source of all desire

Walter Benjamin

The person is no nation
-state to dilettante regarding

sovereignty; the person

does not marshal

their feelings and liken them
to laborers; here metaphors

of the individual fail; in governing
the heart
all is error

placing the heart's nailed box
next to a gesture toward
the built object; gesturing

can be saying things like *I am here by your side*; or
in the soft

sentiment of a hard
moment, to align.

untitled

when I say no one is talking about the grief
of fucking someone

I mean it's everywhere all the time
this murderous anonymity

the relief of uncoupling too obvious

an embarrassment of riches
for the moment between when the fist lands
and the bloom of knowledge that follows

I wanted to grieve the way I wanted to fuck him
the truth is, the truth is too simple for what happened

I needed to lie and to grieve the lie as well

to suckle the child—to feel my body multiply
as if I could feed a waiting crowd

entry

last night the dream was a hot pink slide razor box cutter. the
only one I could find in the office supply store, the mall close
to closing. labor history is the knot of muscle in the meat of
my thumb, ring finger and pinky a claw, curling in to mark
permanent sorrow. labor history is the math of how long a
body part will last under repetitive use. what one cannot
approach without shielding one's eyes. there is work to do
I do not know how to do. I am the monster, the pitiable palm
in need of splitting. poor folks at the office supply did not
realize until it was too late. then we all waited, looking in each
other's eyes. yesterday I laid in the grass in the sun and cried
for want of us. appetite replaces appetite. but of course there
was no vein, no blood. the ways we turn. a celebration of
tulips, the hardening of my hands—shock of recognizable
grief in shared loss. the language of keeping or taking one's
place.

Roden Crater

Whatever the tell says about you

it says about us all. A partial cylinder of light

in the desert is not heaven but it is closer

than even a charitable donation; not burning

a forest does not get you in. Waiting for the wilt

to unwilt is like this man building, for forty

years, his landing strip for aliens. Right now

bare branches have the eggs of all new leaves

inside them—thinking hard about great art

has punitive effects. It makes sense, desiring

to enter strobe as grief display; my only wish

is to see this cylinder before I die. A simple

thing to lie so easily.

untitled

oh pearled body oh sick pearl oh forked pearl of sickness

oh tongue of sadness oh of oh licked asshole oh none

oh clean fork oh split halved oh come came oh bright thread

oh pearled fork oh no oh no oh turned signal oh turn

oh dull brightness oh bright fade oh fate oh hum hum hum

oh meat bird oh weekend traveler oh time turned

oh straight shift oh extinct clam oh irritant oh street

oh sacred thigh oh swish oh swi— oh laundry basket

oh boulders of empathy oh bright tongue oh stroke

oh clean street oh split fork oh facile ending oh slop

oh meat of sickness oh irritating bystander

oh laundered extinction oh halved oh sacred brine

Silent Room

Inherently at cross-purposes, a beam of light cannot excuse

the grain of wood—see, it's math of the heart at its fattiest

why the two together are so satisfying. Violet on a screen

behind orange on a screen makes brown; tertiary is basically

gussied-up brown unless one chooses a discreet method.

The next person who mentions holding space is getting

a punch to the throat. I put off living since I was born.

untitled

I’ve smeared blood on Mondrian

I am not who I thought I was

Brick upon hard noise

My gaping   thinning

To unsatisfactory margins

I don’t believe myself   I believe

Any other significancy

Let me drip the self miserly

Half me halve me have me

Pigs

The goal of psychoanalysis is to help us remove ribs from pigs keeping in mind the line in the show with the character who once gave an equation of suffering greater than death equals the tenderest meat. The goal of psychoanalysis is to help us understand human behavior as a sacrament of the process of becoming human is unfortunately riddled with the holes of becoming human of the unknown stuttering brother of Moses & the angels hear my cry. The goal of psychoanalysis is to snip the frenulum of blue of a nightstick the sky blue of a bleeding mouth the blue of the underside of a thrown brick the blue of wet pavement all of the blue present when the test comes back positive & now your cells have a blue of their own a squashed blue that looks you steadily in the eye as it unbuckles its belt. The goal of psychoanalysis is the same as the word goal if the word goal is the only way to correct action.

untitled

what a disappointment I could not

suck you into me

more readily

or with more resistance

untitled

a house, cursed, is a distraction

open weeping can appear to be
in all things
all things

I know enough theory
to recognize falsehood:

even a virus gone systemic
should be denied agency

every day the loop of isolation grows tighter

love
I haven't bothered to crack that one yet

with a bit of leather between my teeth
hold me under

Effigy

Depth exchanges itself in final moments for a filler

full of what could be but isn't devotion. Seek deconstruction

in worship but practice in craft

the twin: beginning. Cold breaks things. I've lain

in my blood 'til flat on one side, it's the affect

noticeable, written, recorded. How in infancy exposure

increases the likelihood to allergy is the same as white

balloons gathered in effigy and the absence of ourselves

as collateral. So let me tell you—I didn't make it up.

I can lie down anywhere, wake up a Joshua Tree.

false spring

deconstructing the personal into a load bearing transaction is the goal of politic

our bodies are built to bear the single weight for the long term

double in the short unless we en masse into organic immortality

if you haven't learned we are a whetted wedge then remember your position in the midst

what I do with these words does not matter except you are writing the same ones

they act as if it's a dead weight we speak of or a lugging of ashy sentiment

the king-makers will soon dangle by their tongues

we choose our children by feeding them :: theory never outweighs praxis

they see fear in trembling but it's wind that shakes the mock orange leaves

entry

guns are important, heavy, real diamonds

if I could do the job you were meant to do—I would
bring you flowers every night if I could
I would be there if
I could

in service can mean victory to a lot of people
it depends
on what your definition of the word—*is*—is
putting on this collar helps to support
the weight of my
shoulder, readiness is first to readiness

forget
the money we pack time so full it will leak itself dry
the soul is the seat of the matter

can't you see the open
I see my open palm
palm in front of you
in front of you

dear ones, I am writing
to you from this room

it is hot, there is no food
the ground moves always

I love my parents
who love God
who loves everyone
my parents
who love everyone
who should love God
my parents
who work hard to help everyone to love God
who loves everyone
my parents
who help everyone to love themselves
to love each other
my parents
who love God
who love our God
who are giving our God away
my parents
who love God
who see the right thing to do and do it
my parents
who love God
and do not care about oil
my parents
who love God
and do what God tells them to do in order to
save people from themselves
I love my parents
my parents
who have sacrificed so much
who offer so much with open palms

are you beyond my love now?
the river is not clear to drink
but it is what I have

untitled

let it be me
let me step in front of me

a family portrait of me
I should be ashamed of myself

let me take my bullet
let me be the lover of my dreams

let it center on me
let me find the happiness I so richly deserve

falsely accusing myself
let me love unremittingly myself

it wasn't mine to have
let me pick me out of a lineup of me

let me unlock my own potential
in the night I will come for me

let me pay my own bills
let me meditate on myself

where I am the center of my universe
let me fail myself

it all comes down to me
let me give more to me

let me know my true nature
contractually obligated to me

let me deeply grieve the absence of me
let me donate my kidney to me

in the dark about my own motivations
let me be there when I die

watching me when I sleep

Walter Benjamin

here is the pond of water for sitting, getting your drawers wet

walk around with soggy pants

I am the mother who left you there I am that mother that one

in the soggy drawers aftermath

the beak of purity beckons like the plucked vein from a chicken thigh

craft will only take me so far

what is the word to be associated with

the breath of murder blows now on me

reading the ripple, translation is the reflection

the translation is you

o rippled lover! throw your voice on the treetops for the sake of return!

half the face droops

whiskey, chicken casserole, a stick shift stuck in reverse

Fruit

Speak plainly of the purpose of things. A mess

is for cleaning; clean it. What chance is there

for a clean sun? It does not matter even though

it was thought to. Unwrapping the seed of the pit

reveals gasping for air is instead slowly drying

out for years of longest days under a dirty sun.

Stone fruit is a poison. Don't try so hard. Don't

try to find bitter fur.

Objective

Take the foot, for example, as the accessible metaphor

& since it has now been mentioned, spoiled. Conceptual

thought starts as a lie; the permit was paid for just not on

time. The structure of self is that each person packed into

this room needs less space than me; how I wag my

pallbearer's head at any less than full collapse; how there is

purpose to cartography beyond counting the measure.

I almost left! Year of jubilation! My practice of writing

about desire for silence does not bring me closer to the

totality of perfect rest or sincerity—

minor/major/otherwise/in. It was good noodles

under stuttered brown light. My understanding cast itself

into the line drawing we inhabit—pushing, pushing.

Acknowledgments

I would like to extend gratitude for publishing some of these poems, in various forms, to the following: *Afternoon Visitor*, *Annulet*, *Bennington Review*, *Burning House Press*, *Denver Quarterly*, *Guesthouse*, *Hot Pink Magazine*, *Lana Turner*, *mercury firs*, NOIR *SAUNA*, *Paperbag*, *PomPom Lit*, *Prelude*, *Puerto del Sol*, *Seneca Review*, *Sixth Finch*, *The Iowa Review*, *the tiny*, and *West Branch*.

For Enzo, always

This book found its heart during the George Floyd Uprising in PDX 2020. *False Spring* is dedicated to all of us struggling together then and now, and to the people of Palestine.